A Picture Book of
Florence Nightingale

David A. Adler

illustrated by John and Alexandra Wallner

Holiday House / New York

Other books in David A. Adler's *Picture Book Biography* series

A Picture Book of George Washington   *A Picture Book of Eleanor Roosevelt*
A Picture Book of Abraham Lincoln   *A Picture Book of Christopher Columbus*
A Picture Book of Martin Luther King, Jr.   *A Picture Book of John F. Kennedy*
A Picture Book of Thomas Jefferson   *A Picture Book of Simón Bolívar*
A Picture Book of Benjamin Franklin   *A Picture Book of Harriet Tubman*
A Picture Book of Helen Keller   *A Picture Book of Jesse Owens*

*For Robert Stephen
and for Grammie Annie*
D.A.A.

For our friend Cheryl
A.W. & J.W.

Text copyright © 1992 by David A. Adler
Illustrations copyright © 1992 by John and Alexandra Wallner
PRINTED IN THE UNITED STATES OF AMERICA

Library of Congress Cataloging-in-Publication Data

Adler, David A.
A picture book of Florence Nightingale / by David A. Adler :
illustrated by John and Alexandra Wallner. —1st ed.
p.   cm.
Summary: Traces the life of the nineteenth-century English woman
who followed her calling to work in hospitals and improve the
conditions under which the sick were treated.
ISBN 0-8234-0965-1
1. Nightingale, Florence, 1820–1910—Pictorial works—Juvenile
literature. 2. Nurses—England—Biography—Pictorial works—
2. Nurses.] I. Wallner, John, ill. II. Wallner, Alexandra, ill.
III. Title.
RT37.N5A45   1992   91-43388   CIP   AC
610.73'092—dc20
[B]

ISBN 0-8234-1284-9 (pbk.)

ISBN-13: 978-0-8234-0965-5 (hardcover)   ISBN-10: 0-8234-0965-1 (hardcover)
ISBN-13: 978-0-8234-1284-6 (paperback)   ISBN-10: 0-8234-1284-9 (paperback)

Florence Nightingale was born on May 12, 1820, in Florence, Italy. She was named for the city of her birth. Her sister Parthenope was born one year earlier in Naples, Italy. She was named for the city of her birth, too. Parthenope is the Greek name for Naples.

Florence and Parthenope's parents, Fanny and William Nightingale, were from England. Both of their daughters were born while they were traveling in Italy.

The Nightingales were wealthy. They had many servants and lived in a large house near London that they called "Embley Park." They also had a summer home they called "Lea Hurst." Florence and Parthenope were taught by private teachers and by their father.

Florence was a pretty child with an active imagination. She day-dreamed a lot and sometimes thought of herself as a monster or a brave heroine. She was good at her studies, especially math. She also liked to write. She kept a diary, wrote many letters, and was always scribbling notes on scraps of paper.

On July 12, 1830, she wrote after seeing a beautiful sunset, "I thought I loved God then." Almost seven years later, on February 7, 1837, she wrote, "God spoke to me and called me to His service," but she didn't know what this service would be.

In September 1837 the Nightingales traveled to France, Italy, and Switzerland. They attended concerts, operas, and elegant parties. Florence was seventeen then and very popular. Two years later, in 1839, she and her sister were presented to Victoria, the queen of England.

Many men admired Florence. She later said that one man, Richard Monckton Milnes, "was the man I adored." He asked Florence many times to marry him, but she always turned him down.

"I know I could not bear his life," she said. Milnes was a wealthy man and if she married him, she would have to be the same sort of wife her mother was. Florence did not want to spend her time "making society and arranging domestic things."

The 1840s were difficult years in England. People were hungry. Hospitals and prisons were crowded. Florence visited the poor. She brought them food, clothing, and medicine. She helped the sick.

In 1844, at the age of twenty-four, Florence decided her "call" was to work in a hospital—to be a nurse. This was "God's work for me," she wrote. In December 1845 she told this to her parents.

Hospitals then were dirty and smelly. Patients drank whiskey to relieve their pain. Many nurses drank, too. They knew very little about diseases. They were mostly servants who washed the sick and cooked for them. The Nightingales were horrified at Florence's plans. They would not allow their daughter to become a nurse.

Florence was devastated. She became depressed and didn't sleep. She lost weight. On December 5, 1845, she wrote in a letter, "I am dust and nothing, worse than nothing . . . This morning I felt as if my soul would pass away in tears." But Florence did not give up her dream.

Finally, in June 1851, her parents agreed to let her study nursing in Kaiserswerth, Germany. She was thirty-one years old and at last she was beginning her life's work.

Early in 1853 Florence went to Paris, France. There she visited hospitals and watched doctors at work. Later that year she was made the superintendent of The Institution for the Care of Sick Gentlewomen, a small women's hospital in London.

Florence made sure that the hospital was clean. She insisted that it be open to anyone needing care, not just to members of the Church of England.

In 1854, England joined in the Crimean War against Russia. There were not enough hospital beds or doctors for the sick and injured English soldiers. There were no candles, bandages, or nurses. On October 15, 1854, the Secretary At War asked Florence Nightingale to select a group of nurses and take them to the Crimea. Within one week, she was on her way.

Florence was shocked when she arrived in Scutari, Turkey. The hospital was swarming with fleas and rats. Injured soldiers in the hospital were lined up on dirty beds and on the floor.

Florence and the nurses cleaned the hospital, prepared better food, and cared for the sick.

Every night Florence carried a lantern and walked for hours from bed to bed to be sure the soldiers were comfortable.

The soldiers called Florence "The Lady with the Lamp" and looked forward to her visits. As she passed, her shadow fell across their beds, and some reached out to kiss it.

At times Florence worked through the night without sleep. In May 1855 she became sick herself. For two weeks she was near death. She recovered and within a few months was back at work.

Parthenope wrote to Florence that in England, "The people love you." Poems and songs were written about her. Babies were named Florence in her honor. Money was collected for the "Nightingale Fund." Much of it was donated by soldiers. Florence used it later to set up a school for nurses.

The Crimean War ended in March 1856. Great celebrations were planned in Florence Nightingale's honor, but because so many people died in the war, she did not feel like celebrating. She came home quietly and refused to "make a show" of herself.

Florence was thirty-six years old, still a young woman, but her past illness had left her weak. She was very ill again in 1857 and 1861. From then until she died almost fifty years later, she stayed mostly at home where she worked. She was surrounded there with her papers, notebooks, and many pet cats.

Queen Victoria admired Florence and supported her push for improved medical care for British soldiers. A Royal Commission was appointed. Florence gave the commission a 1000 page report, *Notes on Matters Affecting the Health, Efficiency and Hospital Administration of the British Army*. As a result of her work, the living conditions and medical care given British soldiers were improved.

Two books by Florence Nightingale were published in 1859, *Notes on Nursing* and *Notes on Hospitals*. Two years later, in 1861, she advised the United States Secretary of War on setting up army hospitals for those injured in the American Civil War. She also advised on improving health conditions in India.

In 1860 The Nightingale Training School for Nurses was opened in London. Many of Florence's well-trained nurses, called "Nightingales," came for her blessing before they began their work. If a "Nightingale" was sent to some far-off place, Florence sent flowers there to greet the nurse when she arrived.

Nursing schools following the example of the Nightingale School were established in Europe and America.

In 1907, at the age of eighty-seven, Florence Nightingale was awarded the *Order of Merit* by King Edward VII of England. She was the first woman to win the award.

On August 13, 1910, at the age of ninety, Florence Nightingale died quietly in her sleep, but her life's work has survived. She helped make hospitals clean and efficient. She helped make nursing an important, respected profession. Florence Nightingale helped change the world around her into a better, more caring place.

IMPORTANT DATES

1820 Born in Florence, Italy, on May 12.

1837 Wrote in a private note on February 7, "God spoke to me and called me to His service."

1839 Presented to Queen Victoria.

1854 England entered the Crimean War, and Florence Nightingale led a group of nurses to Scutari, Turkey, to care for sick and injured English soldiers.

1856 The Crimean war ended in March. In July, when the last English soldier left the Crimea, she returned to England.

1859 Her books, *Notes on Nursing* and *Notes on Hospitals*, were published.

1860 The Florence Nightingale School of Nurses opened in London, England.

1907 Awarded the *Order of Merit* by King Edward VII.

1910 Died on August 13 in London.